LEVEL C

Finish Line Math Strands

Number and Operations

Continental Press

Acknowledgments

Editorial Development: K.E. Possler

Cover Design: Joan Herring

Interior Design: Earl Cummins, Joan Herring

ISBN 978-0-8454-3992-0

Contents

LESSON 1 Whole Numbers to 1,000

Whole numbers are used to count.

0, 1, 2, 3, 4, 5, ... 10, ... 1,000

You can name whole numbers in different forms.

- **standard form** 419
- **word form** four hundred nineteen

You can show whole numbers with a **model.**

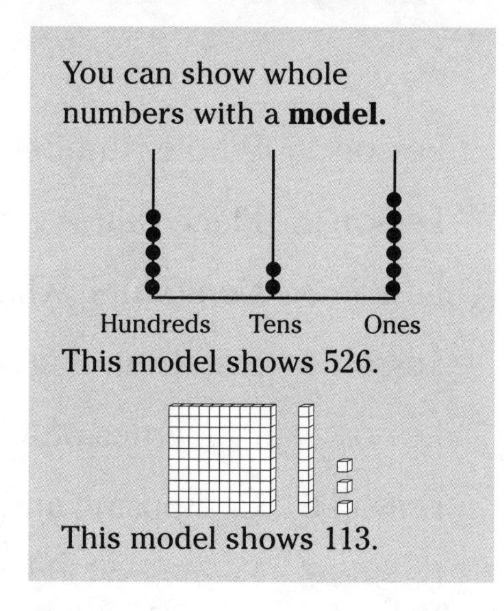

This model shows 526.

This model shows 113.

Read each problem. Circle the letter of the best answer.

1 Look at this sign.

Hikers' Hill
Elevation: 408 feet

What is the elevation, in feet, shown on this sign?

A forty-eight

B four hundred eight

C four hundred eighty

D four thousand eighty

The first digit, 4, is in the hundreds place, so this is written as four hundred. The next digit, 0, means there are 0 tens. The last digit, in the ones place, is written as eight. The number 408 in written form is four hundred eight. The correct answer is B.

2 Nine hundred fifteen tickets were sold to the school play. How is this number written in standard form?

A 95 C 915

B 159 D 950

3 Anita has 76 CDs. How is this number written using words?

A sixty-seven

B seventy-six

C seven hundred six

D seven hundred sixty

4 Glen has six hundred thirty cents in his coin bank. How else can this number be written?

A 63 C 613

B 163 D 630

Read each problem. Write your answers.

5 Marni lives two hundred forty miles from the state capital.

A Write this number in standard form.

Answer: ______________________________

B Explain how you know your answer is correct.

____

____

____

____

6 Jonas has 412 baseball cards in his collection.

A How is this number written using words?

Answer: ______________________________

B Evan has six hundred eight baseball cards in his collection. He wrote this number as 680. Is Evan correct?

Answer: __________

C Explain how you know your answer to part B is correct.

____

____

____

____

Place Value

The value of a digit depends on its place in a number. This is its **place value.**

THOUSANDS	HUNDREDS	TENS	ONES
	5	8	3

In this number, the value of the digit 5 is 5 hundreds, or 500.
The value of the digit 8 is 8 tens, or 80.
The value of the digit 3 is 3 ones, or 3.

A number can be shown in **expanded form.**

5 hundreds + 8 tens + 3 ones =
500 + 80 + 3 = 583

The value of each place is ten times the value of the place to its right.

3 tens
↓
333
↑ ↑
3 hundreds 3 ones

10 ones = 1 ten
10 tens = 1 hundred
10 hundreds = 1 thousand

Read each problem. Circle the letter of the best answer.

1 What is the value of 6 in 164?

A 6

B 16

C 60

D 600

From right to left, the places are the ones, the tens, and the hundreds. The 6 is in the tens place, so its value is 6 tens, or 60. The correct answer is C.

2 The tallest building in the city is 305 feet tall. How is this number written in expanded form?

A 30 + 5

B 300 + 5

C 300 + 50

D 3 + 0 + 5

3 In which number does the 5 have a value of 50?

A 257

B 385

C 504

D 596

4 The number on the sign below is wrong.

Coming Soon!
New Theater:
643 seats

The digits in the ones and tens place were switched. What should the number on the sign be?

A 346

B 436

C 463

D 634

Read each problem. Write your answers.

5 Look at these base 10 blocks. They show a number.

A How is this number written in standard form?

Answer: ____________

B How is this number written in expanded form?

Answer: ____________________________________

6 Megan's house number is shown below.

4 8 6

A How is this number written in expanded form?

Answer: ____________________________________

B Tia thought Megan's house number was different. She wrote the house number in another order to make the ***largest*** possible number with these digits. What number did Tia write?

Answer: ____________

C Explain how you know this is the largest possible number.

____

____

____

Comparing Whole Numbers

To **compare** or **order** whole numbers, look at the digits in the same places, starting on the left.

Jenn has 588 stickers. Lea has 593 stickers. Who has more?

First, line up the numbers. Then start by looking at the digits in the hundreds place.

588 The hundreds digits are the same.
593 So look at the tens digits.

5**8**8 These digits are different.
5**9**3 8 is less than 9.

So, 588 is less than 593, and 593 is greater than 588.

$588 < 593$ or $593 > 588$

Lea has more stickers than Jenn.

The symbol $<$ means "is less than."

$45 < 50$

The symbol $>$ means "is greater than."

$720 > 480$

The symbol ***always*** points toward the smaller number.

Read each problem. Circle the letter of the best answer.

1 Which number goes in the box to make this number sentence true?

$53 < \square$

A 35

B 44

C 49

D 56

The symbol $<$ means "is less than." So you need to find a number that 53 is less than. The number 53 is greater than the numbers in choices A through C. It is less than the number in choice D. The correct answer is D.

2 Which group of numbers is listed in order from ***least to greatest?***

A 545, 455, 554

B 544, 455, 554

C 445, 455, 545

D 454, 445, 554

3 The number of pictures Matt and his friends took one week is listed below.

- Matt took 49 pictures.
- Juan took 65 pictures.
- Tom took 56 pictures.

Which statement is true?

A Matt took fewer pictures than Juan but more than Tom.

B Juan took more pictures than Tom but fewer than Matt.

C Tom took fewer pictures than Juan but more than Matt.

D Juan took more pictures than Matt but fewer than Tom.

Read each problem. Write your answers.

4 Look at these number sentences.

67 ☐ 81   331 ☐ 313   450 ☐ 504

A Write the symbols < or > in the boxes to make each number sentence true.

B Explain how you found each answer.

____

____

____

5 The number of newspapers Sam delivered so far this week is shown in the table below.

NEWSPAPERS DELIVERED THIS WEEK

Day	Number of Newspapers
Monday	105
Tuesday	112
Wednesday	101
Thursday	120

A List these numbers in order from ***least to greatest.***

Answer: ______________________________

B Sam will deliver 111 newspapers on Friday. If he adds this number to the table, where would the number be in your list from part A?

Answer: ______________________________

C Explain how you found your answer.

____

____

____

Skip Counting and Patterns

You can use a **number line** to **skip count.**

To count by 25's, add 25 to a number to find out which number comes next.

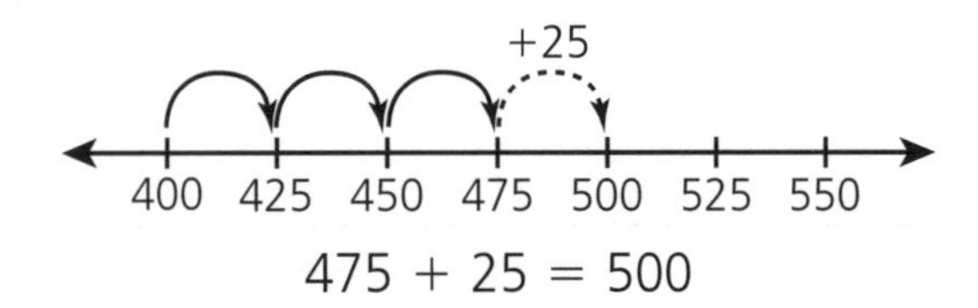

475 + 25 = 500

To count by 50's, keep adding 50.

700 + 50 = 750   750 + 50 = 800   800 + 50 = 850

To count by 100's, keep adding 100.

400, 500, 600, 700, 800, ...

You can skip count by any number.

By 2's:
2, 4, 6, 8, 10, ...

By 3's:
3, 6, 9, 12, 15, ...

By 5's:
5, 10, 15, 20, 25, ...

By 10's:
10, 20, 30, 40, 50, ...

Read each problem. Circle the letter of the best answer.

1 Paula is counting by 100's. If she starts at 450, what will be the ***next*** three numbers she says?

A 500, 550, 600

B 500, 600, 700

C 550, 600, 650

D 550, 650, 750

To find the next three numbers, keep adding 100 to the last number Paula says: 450 + 100 = 550; 550 + 100 = 650; 650 + 100 = 750. The correct answer is D.

2 David is counting by 25's. What is the first number he says after 325?

A 330   **C** 400

B 350   **D** 425

3 Keith is counting by 50's. He starts at the number 275 and ends with 875. Which of these numbers will Keith say?

A 425   **C** 600

B 550   **D** 750

4 Louis uses the number line below to help him count by 50's.

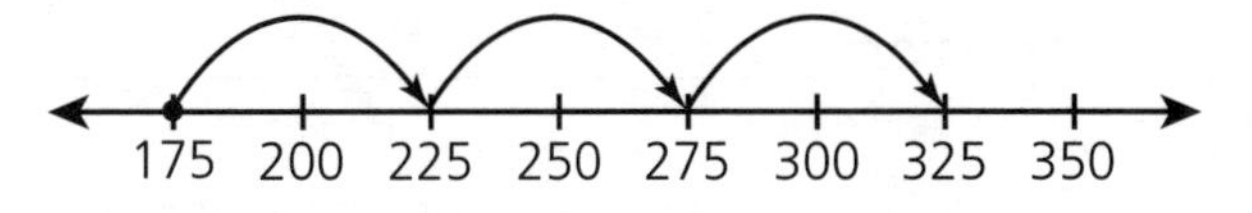

What will be the ***next*** two numbers counted on this number line?

A 350 and 375

B 375 and 475

C 375 and 425

D 400 and 450

Read each problem. Write your answers.

5 Tyler is counting by 25's. He starts at 775 and stops at 900.

A What numbers does Tyler say when counting to 900?

Answer: ______________________________

B Explain how you found your answer.

____

____

____

6 Amy and Beth are counting by 100's.

A Amy starts at 350. What will be the ***next*** three numbers Amy counts?

Answer: ______________________________

B The ***third*** number Beth counts is 475. What is the ***first*** number Beth started counting?

Answer: ____________

C Explain how you found your answer to part B.

____

____

____

Properties of Addition

You can **add** numbers in any **order** and the sum will be the same. This is called the **commutative property.**

▲▲▲ + ▲▲▲▲▲ = ▲▲▲▲▲ + ▲▲▲

$3 + 5 = 8$ $5 + 3 = 8$

So $3 + 5 = 5 + 3$.

You can **group** numbers in any order and **add.** This is called the **associative property.**

$$(8 + 6) + 11 = 8 + (6 + 11)$$
$$14 + 11 = 8 + 17$$
$$25 = 25$$

You ***cannot*** subtract numbers in any order.

$10 - 4$ is ***not*** the same as $4 - 10$.

Parentheses ( ) are grouping symbols. ***Always*** work inside parentheses first.

The associative property is ***not*** true for subtraction.

$$(12 - 7) - 3 \neq 12 - (7 - 3)$$
$$5 - 3 \neq 12 - 4$$
$$2 \neq 8$$

Read each problem. Circle the letter of the best answer.

1 Look at these number sentences.

$10 + \square = 10$ $\square + 5 = 5$

Which statement is true of the missing number in each number sentence?

A It is never 0.

B It is always 0.

C It is always 1.

D It is 5 or 10.

When you add 0 to a number, the number always stays the same: $10 + 0 = 10$ and $0 + 5 = 5$. The missing number is 0. The correct answer is B.

2 Which expression has the same sum as $16 + 11$?

A $16 - 11$

B $11 + 11$

C $16 + 0$

D $11 + 16$

3 Which expression gives the same answer as $(9 + 5) + 2$?

A $9 + (5 + 2)$

B $9 - (5 - 2)$

C $(9 - 5) - 2$

D $(9 + 5) - 2$

4 Which number sentence is true?

A $8 + 0 = 0$

B $6 + 6 = 0$

C $7 + 3 = 3 + 7$

D $9 - 5 = 5 - 9$

Read each problem. Write your answers.

5 Spencer saved $12 and earned $18 more. Marco saved $18 and earned $12 more.

A Who has more money all together, Spencer or Marco?

Answer: ______________________

B Explain how you know your answer is correct.

____

____

____

6 A number is missing from the number sentence below.

$$(\square + 8) + 4 = 9 + (8 + 4)$$

A What number goes in the box to make the number sentence true?

Answer: __________

B Explain how you know your answer is correct.

____

____

____

C What is the value of each side of the number sentence? Use your answer for part A for the number in the box.

Show your work.

Answer: __________

Composing and Decomposing Numbers

A whole number can be **composed** or **decomposed** in many different ways.

$50 + 10 = 60$ $100 - 40 = 60$

$60 = 75 - 15$ $60 = 15 + 15 + 15 + 15$

All of these name the whole number 60.

Compose means "to make up" or "put together."

Decompose means "to take apart" or "break down."

You can use any operation to compose or decompose numbers.

$1 + 1 = 2$
$7 - 5 = 2$
$2 \times 1 = 2$
$8 \div 4 = 2$

Read each problem. Circle the letter of the best answer.

1 Carla bought a box with 500 envelopes. Which expression shows another way of writing 500?

A $2 \times 5 \times 10$

B $600 - 500$

C $100 + 200 + 300$

D $200 + 200 + 50 + 50$

Find the value of each expression. The expression that equals 500 is correct.
$2 \times 5 \times 10 = 10 \times 10 = 100$
$600 - 500 = 100$
$100 + 200 + 300 = 600$
$200 + 200 + 50 + 50 = 500$
The correct answer is D.

2 Which expression shows another way of making $800 - 500$?

A $80 - 50$

B $300 - 100$

C $200 + 300$

D $100 + 100 + 100$

3 Michael's dog weighs 115 pounds. Which expression shows a way of making 115 by adding together three numbers?

A $15 + 15 + 75$

B $15 + 50 + 50$

C $25 + 25 + 75$

D $25 + 40 + 65$

4 Sandi's school was built 60 years ago. Which expression does ***not*** show a way of writing 60?

A $10 + 20 + 30$

B $20 + 20 + 40$

C $90 - 10 - 20$

D $100 - 20 - 20$

Read each problem. Write your answers.

5 A group of 200 people will fly in three airplanes. Show two different ways to make 200 by adding three numbers.

Answer 1: ______________________________

Answer 2: ______________________________

6 Katie, Nora, and Pam are cousins. They live in different cities.

A Katie lives 125 miles from Pam. Use addition to show another way to make 125.

Answer: ______________________________

B Nora lives 245 miles from Pam. Show a way to make 245 by adding three different numbers.

Answer: ______________________________

C Show a way to make 245 by subtracting two numbers from 300.

Answer: ______________________________

Even and Odd Numbers

Even numbers end in 0, 2, 4, 6, or 8.

6, 14, 22, 40, 58, 76 These are all even numbers.

Odd numbers end in 1, 3, 5, 7, or 9.

7, 15, 49, 61, 85, 93 These are all odd numbers.

Every odd number is 1 more than an even number.

$9 = 8 + 1$ $25 = 24 + 1$

Addends are the numbers being added.

$$\begin{array}{r l} 6 & \leftarrow \text{Addend} \\ +5 & \leftarrow \text{Addend} \\ \hline 11 & \leftarrow \text{Sum} \end{array}$$

Read each problem. Circle the letter of the best answer.

1 Which sum is an even number?

A 4 + 3

B 7 + 1

C 5 + 4

D 2 + 9

Choices A, C, and D show the sum of an even number and an odd number, which is always odd. Choice B shows the sum two odd numbers, which is always even. The correct answer is B.

2 Which list shows the odd numbers between 60 and 70?

A 62, 64, 66, 68, 70

B 61, 62, 63, 64, 65

C 61, 63, 65, 67, 69

D 62, 63, 65, 67, 70

3 A list of numbers is below.

421, 455, 459, 463, 489

Which statement is true of these numbers?

A All of the numbers are odd.

B All of the numbers are even.

C There are more odd numbers than even numbers.

D There are more even numbers than odd numbers.

4 Justin had these squares.

□□□□□□□□□□□

He removed some squares and was left with an even number of squares. Which shows a possible number of squares that Justin could have ***removed?***

A □□□

B □□□□□□

C □□

D □□□□

Read each problem. Write your answers.

5 One morning, a bakery sold 57 loaves of bread. The bakery also sold 25 loaves of bread that afternoon.

A Was the total loaves of bread sold that day even or odd?

Answer: ______________________

B Explain how you know your answer is correct.

____

____

____

6 Ms. Lin had a bag of balloons. She gave each of her students 4 balloons. There was 1 balloon left in the bag.

A Was the total number of balloons the students got even or odd?

Answer: ______________________

B Was the total number of balloons even or odd?

Answer: ______________________

C Explain how you found your answers.

____

____

____

____

Adding Three-Digit Numbers

Add numbers by adding the digits in the same places.

First add the ones.

```
 34
+11
---
  5
```

Then add the tens.

```
 34
+11
---
 45
```

When the sum of two digits is 10 or more, **regroup.**

```
   1
 457
+283
----
   0
```

First add the ones: 7 + 3 = 10 ones.
Regroup 10 ones as 1 ten.

```
  11
 457
+283
----
 740
```

Next, add the tens: 1 + 5 + 8 = 14 tens.
Regroup 14 tens as 1 hundred and 4 tens.
Finally, add the hundreds: 1 + 4 + 2 = 7 hundreds.

Add to combine numbers. Add from ***right to left.***

You can add three numbers in any order. The sum is the same.

Read each problem. Circle the letter of the best answer.

1 Find the sum.

```
 564
+288
----
```

A 742
B 752
C 842
D 852

First add the ones: 4 + 8 = 12 ones. Regroup 12 ones as 1 ten and 2 ones. Next, add the tens: 1 + 6 + 8 = 15 tens. Regroup 15 tens as 1 hundred and 5 tens. Finally add the hundreds: 1 + 5 + 2 = 8 hundreds.

```
  11
 564
+288
----
 852
```

The correct answer is D.

2 Which addition problem needs regrouping?

A 341 + 265
B 713 + 246
C 460 + 328
D 851 + 136

3 Which number sentence is true?

A 547 + 185 = 722
B 574 + 185 = 759
C 475 + 158 = 533
D 457 + 158 = 605

4 Find the sum.

```
 144
 593
+216
----
```

A 843
B 853
C 943
D 953

Read each problem. Write your answers.

5 What is the sum of 362 and 361?

Show your work.

Answer: ____________

6 Look at this problem.

$$107 + 498 + 175 = \square$$

A Write the problem in a vertical form below. Then find the sum.

Show your work.

Answer: ____________

B Explain how you used regrouping to find your answer.

____

____

____

More Adding Three-Digit Numbers

To solve addition word problems, first find the numbers to add. Then add the digits in the same places from **right to left.** Regroup if you need to.

When you add, regroup from ***right to left.***

Regroup 13 ones as 1 ten and 3 ones.

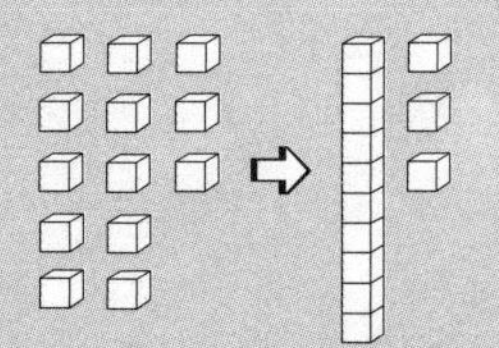

Teddy bowled 2 games. He scored 146 points in his first game. He scored 169 points in his second game. How many points did Teddy score in both games?

The numbers that should be added are 146 and 169. The number 2 is the number of games Teddy played. This is not part of his score, so 2 is not added.

$$\begin{array}{r} {}^{1\,1} \\ 146 \\ +169 \\ \hline 315 \end{array}$$

Add the ones: 6 + 9 = 15. Regroup 15 ones as 1 ten and 5 ones.
Add the tens: 1 + 4 + 6 = 11. Regroup 11 tens as 1 hundred and 1 ten.
Add the hundreds: 1 + 1 + 1 = 3 hundreds.

Read each problem. Circle the letter of the best answer.

1 There are 223 students in grade 3 at North Center School and 314 students in grade 4. How many students are in both grades?

A 537　　**C** 544
B 540　　**D** 547

The numbers 3 and 4 refer to the grades, not the numbers of students. So the only numbers that should be added are 223 and 314. First add the ones: 3 + 4 = 7 ones. Then add the tens: 2 + 1 = 3 tens. Finally, add the hundreds: 2 + 3 = 5 hundreds. There are 537 students. The correct answer is A.

2 Hal has 372 trading cards. Will has 319 trading cards. How many trading cards do they have all together?

A 681　　**C** 691
B 687　　**D** 697

3 Toni bought a CD player for $295 and 8 CDs for $119. How much money did Toni spend on the CD player and CDs?

A $404　　**C** $414
B $412　　**D** $422

4 The table below shows the pounds of apples sold at an orchard in 3 days.

Day	Pounds of Apples
1	187
2	215
3	361

How many pounds of apples were sold in all 3 days?

A 753　　**C** 766
B 763　　**D** 769

Read each problem. Write your answers.

5 Justine played 3 levels of a computer game. Her score in each level is shown below.

Level 1: 435 points
Level 2: 275 points
Level 3: 245 points

How many points did Justine score in all 3 levels?

Show your work.

Answer: ____________

6 The number of seats in each section of a theater is shown in the table at the right.

Section	Number of Seats
1	225
2	176
3	258
4	

The number of seats in section 4 is the same as the number of seats in sections 2 and 3 together.

A How many seats are in section 4?

Show your work.

Answer: ____________

B Explain how you found your answer.

____

____

____

Subtracting Three-Digit Numbers

Subtract numbers by subtracting the digits in the same places. Subtract from **right to left.**

First subtract the ones.

$$\begin{array}{r} 87 \\ -36 \\ \hline 1 \end{array}$$

Then subtract the tens.

$$\begin{array}{r} 87 \\ -36 \\ \hline 51 \end{array}$$

When the digit in a place is not large enough to subtract from, regroup the next place to the **left.**

$$\begin{array}{r} {}^{5\,11} \\ 7\not{6}\not{1} \\ -154 \\ \hline 7 \end{array}$$

The digit in the ones place, 1, is less than 4, so regroup 6 tens as 5 tens and 10 ones. Now subtract the ones: 11 − 4 = 7 ones.

$$\begin{array}{r} {}^{5\,11} \\ 7\not{6}\not{1} \\ -154 \\ \hline 607 \end{array}$$

Subtract the tens: 5 − 5 = 0 tens. Subtract the hundreds: 7 − 1 = 6 hundreds.

Subtract to
- compare numbers
- find how many are left
- find a missing part

Addition and subtraction are opposite operations. You can add to check subtraction.

16 − 7 = 9 because 9 + 7 = 16.

Read each problem. Circle the letter of the best answer.

1 Find the difference.

$$\begin{array}{r} 627 \\ -169 \\ \hline \end{array}$$

A 458 **C** 542

B 468 **D** 568

To subtract 169 from 627, first regroup 2 tens as 1 ten and 10 ones. Now there are a total of 17 ones. Subtract the ones. Then regroup 6 hundreds as 5 hundreds and 10 tens. Then subtract the tens and then the hundreds.

$$\begin{array}{r} {}^{11} \\ {}^{5\,\not{1}\,17} \\ \not{6}\not{2}\not{7} \\ -169 \\ \hline 458 \end{array}$$

The correct answer is A.

2 Which subtraction problem needs regrouping?

A 518 − 307 **C** 628 − 525

B 766 − 271 **D** 851 − 340

3 Find the difference.

674 − 331 = □

A 303 **C** 343

B 335 **D** 345

4 Which number sentence is true?

A 614 − 227 = 413

B 461 − 227 = 246

C 614 − 272 = 442

D 461 − 272 = 189

Read each problem. Write your answers.

5 What is the difference between 890 and 437?

Show your work.

Answer: ____________

6 Look at this problem.

$$603 - 375 = \square$$

A Write the problem in a vertical form below. Then find the difference.

Show your work.

Answer: ____________

B Explain how you used regrouping to find your answer.

____

____

____

LESSON 11 More Subtracting Three-Digit Numbers

To solve subtraction word problems, first find the numbers to subtract. Write the problem. Then subtract the digits in the same places from **right to left.** Regroup if you need to.

Fern collected 270 stamps. Lisa collected 163 stamps. How many more stamps did Fern collect than Lisa?

Subtract 163 from 270. Subtract digits from right to left.

```
  6 10
 2 7 0     Regroup 7 tens as 6 tens and 10 ones.
−1 6 3     Subtract the ones, the tens, and the hundreds
 1 0 7     digits.
```

When you subtract, regroup from ***left to right.***

Regroup 3 tens as 2 tens and 10 ones.

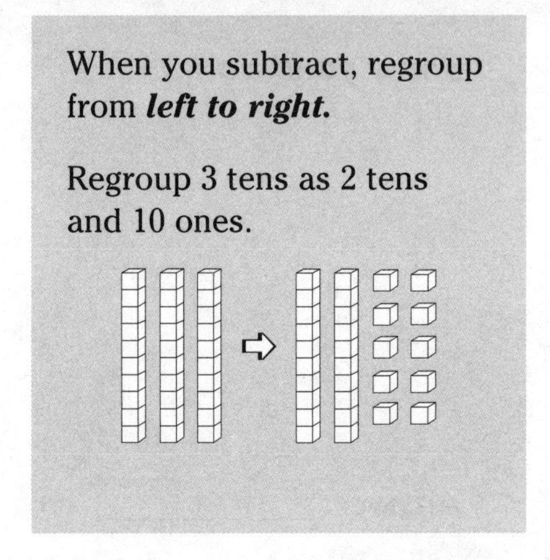

Read each problem. Circle the letter of the best answer.

1 There were 472 children on a field trip. If there were 255 boys, how many girls were there?

A 213 **C** 223

B 217 **D** 227

Subtract 255 from 472. First regroup 7 tens as 6 tens and 10 ones. Subtract the ones, then the tens, and then the hundreds.

```
  6 12
 4 7 2
−2 5 5
 2 1 7
```

The correct answer is B.

2 Julio saved $550 for a new bike. If the bike costs $229, how much money will Julio have left?

A $321

B $329

C $331

D $339

3 The heights, in meters, of some skyscrapers are shown in the table below.

Skyscraper	Height (meters)
Sears Tower	442
Key Tower	289
Empire State Building	381

How much taller is the Sears Tower than the Key Tower?

A 61 meters **C** 165 meters

B 153 meters **D** 247 meters

4 Li's dog weighs 133 pounds. Dan's dog weighs 69 pounds. How much heavier is Li's dog than Dan's dog?

A 64 pounds

B 66 pounds

C 74 pounds

D 76 pounds

Read each problem. Write your answers.

5 The regular price of a computer is $970. This week it is on sale for $789. How much money is saved by buying the computer this week?

Show your work.

Answer: ____________

6 Peter hit a golf ball 4 times. The number of yards each golf ball went is shown in the table below.

Golf Ball	Number of Yards
1	126
2	119
3	122
4	160

A What is the difference in yards between the farthest distance and the shortest distance?

Show your work.

Answer: ____________

B Explain how you found your answer.

____

____

____

Meaning of Multiplication

Multiplication is like repeated addition. You can use an **array** or other model to show multiplication.

Cody, Ryan, and Hiro each ate 5 crackers. How many crackers did they eat in all?

This array shows 3 rows of 5 crackers.

O O O O O
O O O O O
O O O O O

$$5 + 5 + 5 = 3 \text{ rows of } 5$$
$$3 \times 5 = 15$$

They ate 15 crackers in all.

Factors are the numbers you multiply to get a product.

$$\begin{array}{r l} 2 & \leftarrow \text{Factor} \\ \times 7 & \leftarrow \text{Factor} \\ \hline 14 & \leftarrow \text{Product} \end{array}$$

Read each problem. Circle the letter of the best answer.

1 Which number sentence shows the model below?

A $3 \times 5 = \square$

B $3 \times 6 = \square$

C $4 \times 5 = \square$

D $4 \times 6 = \square$

> The model shows 3 rows of 6 shapes each. This is the same as $3 \times 6 = \square$. The correct answer is B.

2 Which multiplication expression is modeled below?

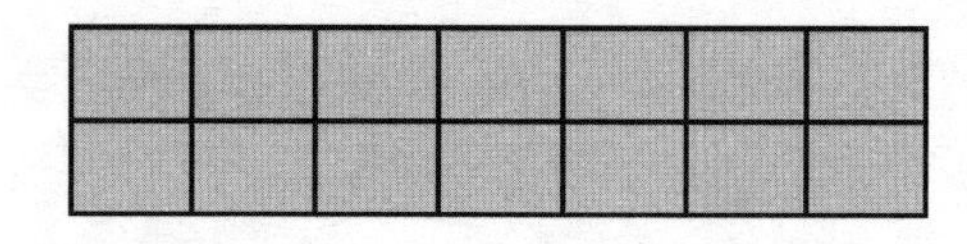

A 1×7

B 1×8

C 2×7

D 2×8

3 Sela bought 6 packs of gum. Each pack had 5 pieces of gum. Which model shows the total pieces of gum Sela bought?

A

B

C

D

Read each problem. Write your answers.

4 Nick built 5 toy wagons. He put 4 wheels on each wagon.

A Draw a picture to model the total number of wheels Nick put on these wagons.

B Write a number sentence to show the total number of wheels Nick put on these wagons.

Answer: ______________________________

5 Mary, Julia, and Vicki each collected 8 half-dollar coins.

A Draw a picture to model the total number of half-dollar coins Mary, Julia, and Vicki have.

B How many half-dollar coins are there in all?

Answer: __________

C Explain why your answer is correct.

____

____

____

Multiplication Facts

Multiply to combine groups of equal size.

Kara has 4 boxes of 8 crayons. How many crayons does she have in all?

$8 + 8 + 8 + 8 = 32$ crayons
$4 \times 8 = 32$ crayons

Kara has 32 crayons in all.

Multiplication is like repeated addition.

$3 + 3 + 3 + 3 = 4 \times 3$

Read each problem. Circle the letter of the best answer.

1 Charlie walked 3 miles on Monday, Tuesday, Wednesday, Thursday, and Friday. How many miles did he walk in all?

A 5
B 8
C 12
D 15

Charlie walked the same number of miles, 3, on each of 5 days. Multiply to find the number of miles he walked in all: $5 \times 3 = 15$. The correct answer is D.

2 Seth bought 6 sandwiches for his friends. Each sandwich cost $7. How much did Seth spend on the sandwiches?

A $13
B $42
C $48
D $67

3 Which number sentence has a product of 24?

A $6 \times 3 = \square$
B $7 \times 4 = \square$
C $8 \times 3 = \square$
D $9 \times 4 = \square$

4 It takes Hannah 2 minutes to read a page in a book. Which number sentence can be used to show the number of minutes it takes Hannah to read 9 pages?

A $2 + 9 = \square$
B $9 \times 2 = \square$
C $9 \div 2 = \square$
D $2 \div 9 = \square$

Read each problem. Write your answers.

5 Vijay pays $8 for a singing lesson.

A How much will Vijay pay for 7 singing lessons?

Answer: ____________

B Explain how you found your answer.

____

____

____

6 Tess has 4 ribbons that are each 7 inches long. Leah has 7 ribbons that are each 4 inches long.

A How many inches of ribbon does Tess have?

Answer: ____________

B Who has more inches of ribbon, Tess or Leah?

Show your work.

Answer: ________________________

C Explain why your answer is correct.

____

____

____

Properties of Multiplication

You can **multiply** numbers in any **order.** The product is the same. This is called the **commutative property.**

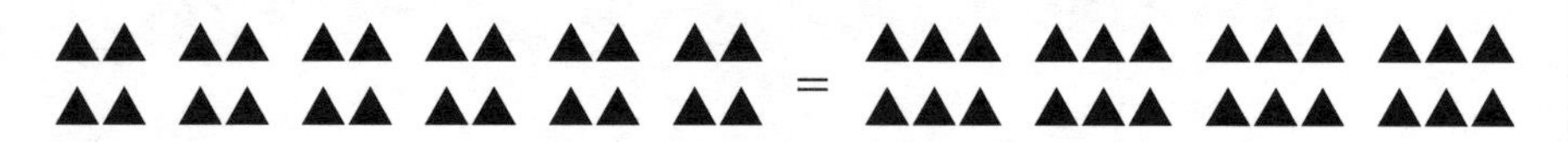

$6 \times 4 = 24$ $4 \times 6 = 24$

So $6 \times 4 = 4 \times 6$.

You can **multiply or divide a number by 1.** The number stays the same.

$7 \times 1 = 7$ $12 \div 1 = 12$

You can **multiply a number by 0.** The product will be 0. It does not matter what order the numbers are in.

$3 \times 0 = 0$ $0 \times 8 = 0$

Multiplication and division are inverse operations.

You ***cannot*** divide numbers in any order.

$10 \div 2$ is ***not*** the same as $2 \div 10$.

When you divide any number by itself, the quotient is 1.

$8 \div 8 = 1$

When you divide any number by 1, the quotient is the number.

$8 \div 1 = 8$

Read each problem. Circle the letter of the best answer.

1 Which number sentence describes both pictures below?

A $6 + 2 = 2 + 6$

B $6 \times 2 = 2 + 6$

C $6 \times 2 = 2 \times 6$

D $6 \times 6 = 2 \times 2$

The pictures show 6 groups of 2 stars each and 2 groups of 6 stars each. This models multiplication. You can multiply numbers in any order. The product is the same. Choice A is wrong since it shows addition. Choice B is wrong since 12 does not equal 8. Choice D is wrong since 36 does not equal 4. The correct answer is C since 12 equals 12.

2 What number goes in the box to make this number sentence true?

$\square \times 4 = 4$

A 0 **C** 4

B 1 **D** 8

3 Look at these number sentences.

$5 \times \square = 0$ $\square \times 10 = 0$

Which statement is true about the missing number in each number sentence?

A It is always 0. **C** It is always 1.

B It is never 0. **D** It is 5 or 10.

4 Which of these number sentences is true?

A $8 \times 0 = 8$ **C** $0 \times 8 = 8$

B $8 \times 1 = 1$ **D** $1 \times 8 = 8$

Read each problem. Write your answers.

5 A number sentence is below.

$$12 \times \square = 12$$

A What number goes in the box to make this number sentence true?

Answer: ____________

B Explain how you know your answer is correct.

____

____

____

6 Marvin bought 4 packs of 3 juice boxes. Dennis bought 3 packs of 4 juice boxes.

A Draw pictures to show this number sentence.

4 groups of 3 = 3 groups of 4

Marvin's Juice Boxes	Dennis's Juice Boxes

B Who bought more juice boxes, Marvin or Dennis?

Answer: ________________________

C Explain why your answer is correct.

____

____

____

LESSON 15 Multiplication Facts to 12×12

Multiply whole numbers from **right to left.** Multiply the ones. Then multiply the tens.

> You can use visual models to show multiplication and division.
> - array
> - area model
> - patterns or rules
>
> The word ***double*** means to multiply by 2. The word ***triple*** means to multiply by 3.

Sandy's family bought 5 all-day ride passes to the school fair. Each ride pass cost \$14. How much did Sandy's family spend?

$$\begin{array}{r} {}^{2}\\ \$14 \\ \times 5 \\ \hline \$70 \end{array}$$

Multiply the ones: $5 \times 4 = 20$ ones. Write the 0 in the ones place.
Regroup 20 ones as 2 tens and write it above the tens place.
Multiply the tens: $5 \times 1 = 5$ tens. Add the 2 tens for 7 tens.

Sandy's family spent \$70 on ride passes.

Read each problem. Circle the letter of the best answer.

1 Each car on a roller coaster holds 6 people. The roller coaster has 12 cars. What is the greatest number of people that can ride the roller coaster at one time?

A 18 **C** 72
B 48 **D** 82

> There are 12 cars on the roller coaster that hold 6 people. Multiply to find the greatest number of people that can ride the roller coaster. First, multiply the ones: $6 \times 2 = 12$ ones. Regroup 12 ones as 1 ten and 2 ones. Write the 2 in the ones place. Write the 1 above the tens place. Then multiply the tens: $6 \times 1 = 6 + 1 = 7$ tens.
>
> $$\begin{array}{r} {}^{1}\\ 12 \\ \times 6 \\ \hline 72 \end{array}$$
>
> The correct answer is C.

2 Sasha has 10 charms for her bracelet. Diane has triple the number of charms as Sasha. How many charms does Diane have?

A 3 **C** 30
B 20 **D** 50

3 Find the product.

$$\begin{array}{r} 11 \\ \times 7 \\ \hline \end{array}$$

A 17 **C** 71
B 18 **D** 77

4 Which expression does this model show?

❀ ❀ ❀ ❀ ❀ ❀ ❀ ❀ ❀ ❀ ❀ ❀
❀ ❀ ❀ ❀ ❀ ❀ ❀ ❀ ❀ ❀ ❀ ❀
❀ ❀ ❀ ❀ ❀ ❀ ❀ ❀ ❀ ❀ ❀ ❀

A 3×12 **C** 3×36
B $12 \div 3$ **D** $36 \div 3$

Read each problem. Write your answers.

5 Logan has 5 boxes of thank-you cards. Each box has 12 thank-you cards.

A How many thank-you cards does Logan have in all?

Answer: ____________

B Explain how you found your answer.

____

____

____

6 For a school concert, students are lined up in rows of 12. There are a total of 11 rows.

A How many children are lined up for the concert?

Show your work.

Answer: ____________

B In the space below, draw an array to show the lines of children formed for the concert.

LESSON 16 Meaning of Division

Division is like repeated subtraction. You can use an **array** or other model to show division.

Juan put 45 snowflakes in 5 equal rows on the wall. How many snowflakes are in each row?

$$45 \div 5 = 9 \qquad 5\overline{)45} = 9$$

There are 9 snowflakes in each row.

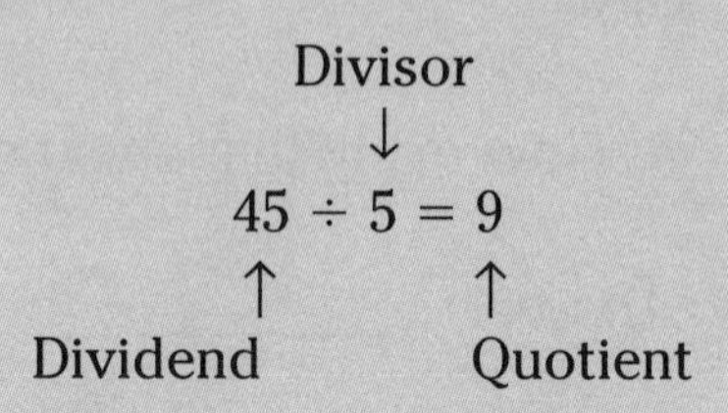

Divisor ↓ $45 \div 5 = 9$ ↑ Dividend ↑ Quotient

Multiplication and division are opposite operations. You can use multiplication to check division.

$45 \div 5 = 9$ because $9 \times 5 = 45$.

The word ***halve*** means divide by 2.

Read each problem. Circle the letter of the best answer.

1 Which model shows $18 \div 6 = 3$?

A 

B 

C 

D 

The model for $18 \div 6 = 3$ shows 18 ■'s in 6 equal groups. Each group has 3 ■'s. Choices A, B, and C don't show 18 ■'s in groups of 3 ■'s. The correct answer is D.

2 Which division expression is modeled below?

★ ★ ★ ★	★ ★ ★ ★	★ ★ ★ ★	★ ★ ★ ★	★ ★ ★ ★

A $20 \div 4 = 5$

B $20 \div 5 = 5$

C $25 \div 4 = 5$

D $25 \div 5 = 5$

3 Steven put 36 marbles in bags. He put 6 marbles in each bag. Which model can be used to show the number of bags of marbles Steven has?

A 

B 

C 

D 

Read each problem. Write your answers.

4 Anna put 30 eggs into cartons that hold 6 eggs each.

A Draw a picture to model the total number of egg cartons Anna used to hold these 30 eggs.

B Write a number sentence to show the total number of egg cartons Anna used to hold these eggs.

Answer: ____________________________________

5 Mr. Carson hung pictures on a wall forming this design.

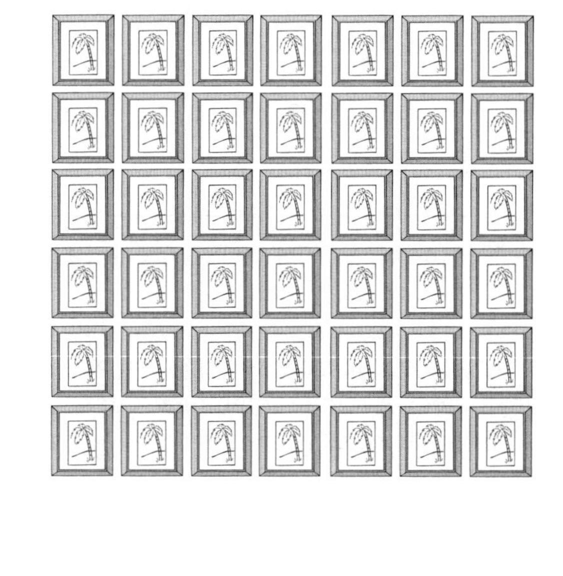

A Write a multiplication fact to match the design of pictures Mr. Carson hung on his wall.

Answer: ____________________________________

B Write a division fact to match the design of pictures Mr. Carson hung on his wall.

Answer: ____________________________________

C Explain how you found your answers.

____

____

____

Division Facts

Divide to break a group into groups of equal size.

A case contains 48 granola bars. There are 6 boxes of granola bars in the case. How many granola bars are in each box?

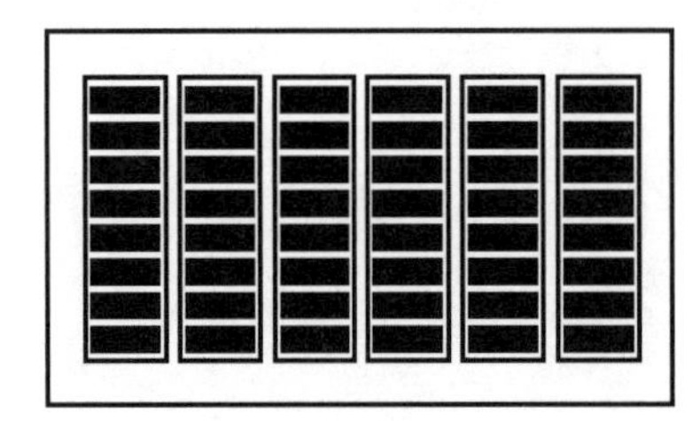

$48 \div 6 = 8$ granola bars

$$\begin{array}{r} 8 \\ 6\overline{)48} \\ \underline{48} \end{array}$$

Another way to show division is with a fraction.

$$\frac{21}{7} = 3$$

means the same as $21 \div 7 = 3$.

Read each problem. Circle the letter of the best answer.

1 Six friends shared 12 slices of pizza. Each friend ate the same number of pizza slices. Which number sentence shows how many pizza slices each friend ate?

A $12 + 6 = 18$

B $12 - 6 = 6$

C $12 \times 6 = 72$

D $12 \div 6 = 2$

The problem asks you to break 12 slices of pizza into six equal groups for 6 friends. Division is the only operation that allows you to break things into equal groups. Choices A and C combine groups. Choice B shows what is left when 6 is taken away. The correct answer is D.

2 A box contains 56 greeting cards in 8 different designs. There are the same number of cards in each design. Which number sentence can be solved to find the number of cards of each design?

A $56 \times 8 = \square$

B $56 \div 8 = \square$

C $56 + 8 = \square$

D $56 - 8 = \square$

3 Which number sentence has an answer of 4?

A $35 \div 9 = \square$

B $32 \div 8 = \square$

C $21 \div 7 = \square$

D $30 \div 6 = \square$

4 Divide.

$72 \div 9 =$

A 4

B 6

C 7

D 8

Read each problem. Write your answers.

5 Terry bought 4 pounds of fish for $24.

A What is the price for each pound of fish Terry bought?

Answer: ____________

B Explain how you found your answer.

____

____

____

6 Rachel set up 36 chairs with 4 chairs in each row.

A How many rows of chairs did Rachel set up?

Show your work.

Answer: ____________

B Lydia set up 36 chairs with 6 chairs in each row. How many ***fewer*** rows of chairs did Lydia set up than Rachel?

Show your work.

Answer: ____________

C Explain why your answer to part B is correct.

____

____

____

Choosing the Operation

To solve word problems, it is important to know which **operation** to choose.

Clare got 29 emails last week. She got 45 emails this week. How many emails did Clare get both weeks?

$$\begin{array}{r} {}^{1}\\ 29 \\ +45 \\ \hline 74 \end{array}$$

Add the emails Clare got both weeks.

She got 74 emails both weeks.

In 6 days, Ms. Wilton gave 30 singing lessons. She gave the same number of lessons each day. How many lessons did Ms. Wilton give each day?

$$\begin{array}{r} 5 \\ 6\overline{)30} \\ \underline{30} \end{array}$$

Divide the number of lessons by the number of days.

She gave 5 lessons each day.

Subtract to
- compare numbers
- find how many are left
- find a missing part

$$\begin{array}{rl} 300 & \leftarrow \text{Minuend} \\ -\ 21 & \leftarrow \text{Subtrahend} \\ \hline 279 & \leftarrow \text{Difference} \end{array}$$

Multiply to combine groups of equal size.

$$\begin{array}{rl} 3 & \leftarrow \text{Factor} \\ \times 5 & \leftarrow \text{Factor} \\ \hline 15 & \leftarrow \text{Product} \end{array}$$

Read each problem. Circle the letter of the best answer.

1 Taylor rode her bike 4 days this week. Each of these days she rode 8 miles. Which operation would she use to find out the total number of miles she rode her bike this week?

A addition
B subtraction
C multiplication
D division

Taylor rode the same number of miles each day. To find the total miles, combine groups. Multiplication is used to combine groups of equal size. The correct answer is C.

2 Keisha is 60 inches tall. Martha is 6 inches taller than Keisha. Which number sentence can be used to find Martha's height in inches?

A $60 + 6 = \square$
B $60 - 6 = \square$
C $60 \times 6 = \square$
D $60 \div 6 = \square$

3 Tim, Doug, Troy, and Ray won a total of 24 tokens. Each boy shared the tokens equally. Which operation should be used to find how many tokens each boy got?

A addition
B subtraction
C multiplication
D division

4 Janis scored 88 points on a spelling test. This is 4 points more than Ashley scored. Which number sentence can be used to find the points Ashley scored on the spelling test?

A $88 + 4 = \square$
B $88 - 4 = \square$
C $88 \times 4 = \square$
D $88 \div 4 = \square$

Read each problem. Write your answers.

5 Nathan earned $45 raking leaves for 5 hours. He earned the same dollar amount each hour.

A Write a number sentence that can be used to find the amount Nathan earned each hour.

Answer: ______________________________

B Explain why you chose that operation.

____

____

____

6 Ms. Smith wrote these statements on the chalkboard:

1. Alex played piano 15 minutes on each of 5 days.
2. Greg played piano 15 minutes one day and 5 minutes another day.

A Which operation can be used to find the total minutes each person played the piano?

Alex: ______________________________

Greg: ______________________________

B Who played the piano longer, Alex or Greg?

Show your work.

Answer: ____________________

C Explain why your answer to part B is correct.

____

____

____

Rounding Numbers and Estimating

To **round** a whole number to a particular place, look at the digit in the ***next*** place to the right. If it is 4 or less, round down. If it is 5 or greater, round up.

To round a number to the **nearest ten,** look at the ones.

What is 63 to the nearest ten?
Look at the ones: ↓
63
3 is less than 5, so round down to 60.

To round a number to the **nearest hundred,** look at the tens.

What is 251 to the nearest hundred?
Look at the tens: ↓
251
5 is 5 or greater, so round up to 300.

If the digit is:

0 1 2 3 4	5 6 7 8 9
⟵	⟶
round down	round up

When you round a number, replace any digit ***below*** the place you are rounding to with a zero.

574
570 → to the nearest ten, use a zero for the ones place
600 → to the nearest hundred, use zeros for the ones and tens places

---

Read each problem. Circle the letter of the best answer.

1 Which number would ***not*** round to 100?

A 50
B 61
C 147
D 160

Round each number to the nearest hundred. Look at the digit in the tens place. If it is 4 or less, round down. If it is 5 or greater, round up. In choice A, 50 rounds up to 100. In choice B, 61 rounds up to 100. In choice C, 147 rounds down to 100. In choice D, 160 rounds up to 200. The correct answer is D.

2 Which statement is true when rounding to the nearest hundred?

A 211 becomes 210
B 254 becomes 300
C 333 becomes 400
D 345 becomes 400

3 Which situation is best measured with an estimate?

A the cost of a postage stamp
B the number of pencils in a box
C the number of bananas in a bunch
D the distance from Chicago to Dallas

4 Which situation is best for Jane to measure with an estimate?

A the number of fish in her fish tank
B the number of buttons on her sweater
C the number of hours of sleep she got last night
D the number of homework problems she has in math

Read each problem. Write your answers.

5 These numbers are written on a piece of paper:

140 159 191 195 205 212 244

Malcolm rounded each of these numbers to the nearest ten.

A Which number or numbers rounded to 200?

Answer: ______________________

B Explain how you know your answer is correct.

____

____

____

6 There are 376 students in grade 3.

A What is this number rounded to the nearest ten students?

Answer: ___________

B What is this number rounded to the nearest hundred students?

Answer: ___________

C Grade 4 has a different number of students than grade 3. The number of students in grade 4 rounded to the nearest ten is the same number that grade 3 rounds to. What are all the possible numbers of students in grade 4?

Answer: ____

Estimating Sums and Differences

To **estimate** a **sum** or **difference,** first round the numbers. Then add or subtract.

There are 486 seats in a cafeteria. Of these, 194 seats are filled. ***About*** how many seats in the cafeteria are empty?

Round to the nearest hundred. Then subtract.

486 rounds to 500
−194 rounds to 200
about 300

There are ***about*** 300 empty seats in the cafeteria.

You can round numbers to the nearest ten or the nearest hundred, depending on how accurate the estimate must be.

You can use estimation to decide if an answer is reasonable.

Read each problem. Circle the letter of the best answer.

1 Dale drove 184 miles on Saturday. He drove 112 miles Sunday. Which is the ***most*** reasonable estimate for how much farther Dale drove Saturday?

A 60 miles
B 70 miles
C 80 miles
D 100 miles

Round to the nearest ten. Then subtract. 184 rounds down to 180 and 112 rounds down to 110: 180 − 110 = 70. A reasonable estimate would be 70 miles. The correct answer is B.

2 Nina earned $36 on Sunday, $18 on Tuesday, and $25 on Friday. She estimates that she earned about $60 all together. Is her estimate reasonable?

A Yes, she earned ***about*** $60.
B No, she earned ***about*** $70.
C No, she earned ***about*** $80.
D No, she earned ***about*** $90.

3 There are 236 crayons and 155 markers in the art room. Which is the ***most*** reasonable estimate for the total number of crayons and markers?

A between 300 and 325
B between 325 and 350
C between 350 and 375
D between 375 and 400

4 A bakery made 276 vanilla cupcakes. It made 408 chocolate cupcakes. Ashana estimates that there are about 130 more chocolate cupcakes than vanilla cupcakes. Is her estimate reasonable?

A Yes, the answer should be ***about*** 130.
B No, the answer should be ***about*** 110.
C No, the answer should be ***about*** 120.
D No, the answer should be ***about*** 140.

Read each problem. Write your answers.

5 Tanya jumped rope 84 times without stopping. Sharon jumped rope 113 times without stopping. Sharon estimates that she jumped rope about 30 jumps more than Tanya.

A Is Sharon's estimate reasonable?

Answer: ____________

B Explain how you know your answer is correct.

____

____

____

6 Vern spent $18 for a new shirt and $59 for a new jacket. He estimates that he spent about $95 in all.

A Is Vern's estimate reasonable?

Answer: ____________

B Explain how you know your answer is correct.

____

____

____

C Suppose Vern paid with $100. How could you estimate the amount of change Vern would get back ?

____

____

____

LESSON 21 Understanding Fractions

A fraction can name part of a whole. To name a fraction, write the number of parts talked about as the **numerator.** Write the number of equal parts in the whole as the **denominator.**

Three-fourths = $= \frac{3}{4}$ ← Numerator ← Denominator

This rectangle has 3 shaded parts. It has 4 equal parts in all. The fraction $\frac{3}{4}$ names the shaded part of the whole rectangle.

A fraction can name part of a **set.**

There are 3 happy faces. There are 4 faces all together. So $\frac{3}{4}$ of the faces are happy.

The parts of a fraction must be equal in size.

These are thirds. 

These are *not* thirds. 

A **unit fraction *always*** has 1 for a numerator. These are examples of unit fractions:

One-half $\frac{1}{2}$

One-third $\frac{1}{3}$

One-sixth $\frac{1}{6}$

One-tenth $\frac{1}{10}$

Read each problem. Circle the letter of the best answer.

1 Sara has these crayons.

RED GREEN PINK
BLUE PEACH PURPLE

She used $\frac{1}{2}$ of the crayons to color a picture. How many crayons did Sara use?

A 1

B 2

C 3

D 6

There are 6 crayons. The fraction $\frac{1}{2}$ is the same as dividing into 2 equal groups. So each group would have 3 crayons. The correct answer is C.

2 Which fraction has a numerator of 3 and a denominator of 5?

A $\frac{2}{3}$

B $\frac{1}{5}$

C $\frac{3}{5}$

D $\frac{5}{3}$

3 Libby has these cards.

What fraction of these cards show squares?

A $\frac{1}{5}$

B $\frac{2}{5}$

C $\frac{1}{4}$

D $\frac{1}{2}$

4 Which shape is divided into fourths?

A 

B 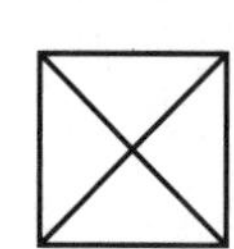

C 

D 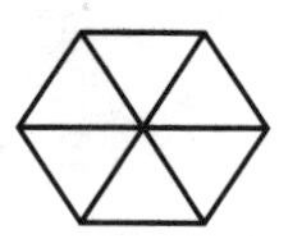

Read each problem. Write your answers.

5 Zack has these coins.

A What fraction of these coins are nickels?

Answer: ____________

B Explain how you found your answer.

____

____

____

6 The rectangle below is divided into 8 equal sections.

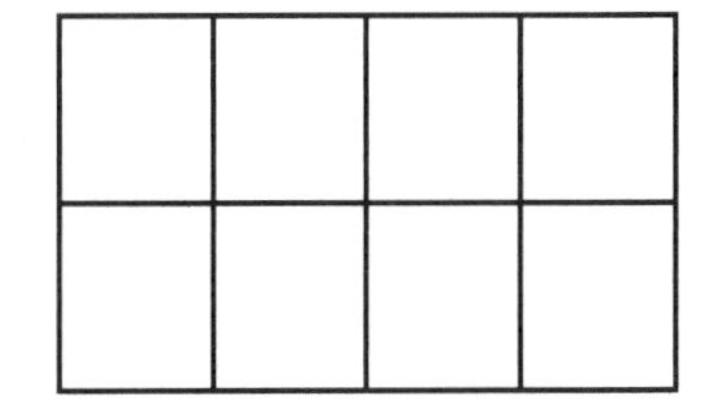

A Shade $\frac{1}{4}$ of this rectangle.

B What fraction of the rectangle is ***not*** shaded?

Answer: ____________

C Explain how you know your answer is correct.

____

____

____

Comparing and Ordering Fractions

Equivalent fractions name the same number in different terms.

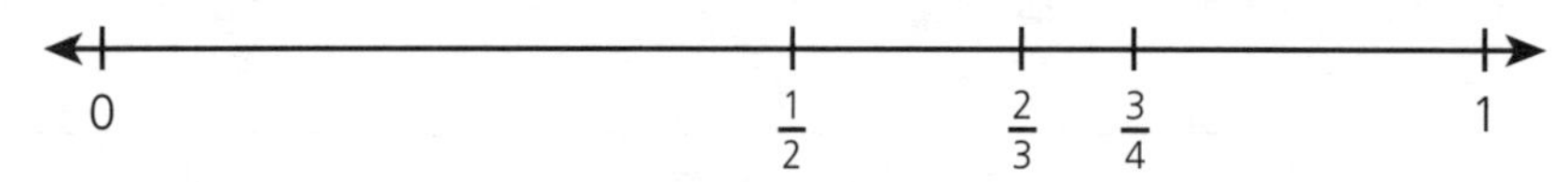

$\frac{1}{3} = \frac{2}{6}$

The fractions $\frac{1}{3}$ and $\frac{2}{6}$ are equivalent.

$\frac{3}{4}$ ← Numerator
4 ← Denominator

When the numerator and denominator are the same digit, the fraction is equal to 1.

$\frac{4}{4} = 1 \quad \frac{7}{7} = 1$

You can use a number line to **compare** fractions. Numbers on the left are ***always*** smaller than numbers on the right.

0 — $\frac{1}{2}$ — $\frac{2}{3}$ — $\frac{3}{4}$ — 1

The fraction $\frac{3}{4}$ is to the right of $\frac{1}{2}$ and $\frac{2}{3}$. So $\frac{3}{4}$ is the largest fraction and $\frac{1}{2}$ is the smallest.

Read each problem. Circle the letter of the best answer.

1 Which point is located at $\frac{1}{3}$ on the number line below?

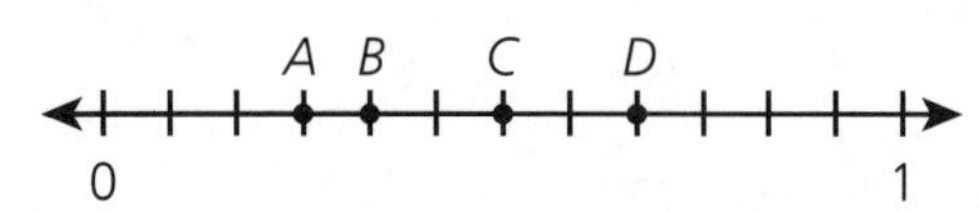

A point *A* **C** point *C*

B point *B* **D** point *D*

This number line is divided into 12 equal sections. The fraction $\frac{1}{3}$ is equivalent to the fraction $\frac{4}{12}$. The point that marks the fourth section on the number line is *B*. The correct answer is B.

2 Zoe practiced yoga for $\frac{1}{2}$ hour today. What fraction equals $\frac{1}{2}$?

A $\frac{1}{3}$ **C** $\frac{3}{6}$

B $\frac{2}{6}$ **D** $\frac{2}{3}$

3 Jesse read $\frac{1}{4}$ of a book on Friday, $\frac{1}{3}$ of the book on Saturday, $\frac{3}{12}$ of the book Sunday, and the rest on Monday. Which statement is true?

A Jesse read more of the book on Friday than on Sunday.

B Jesse read more of the book on Sunday than on Friday.

C Jesse read more of the book on Friday than on Saturday.

D Jesse read more of the book on Saturday than on Friday.

4 Henry finished $\frac{4}{6}$ of his homework. What fraction equals $\frac{4}{6}$?

A $\frac{2}{3}$ **C** $\frac{1}{2}$

B $\frac{1}{3}$ **D** $\frac{2}{8}$

Read each problem. Write your answers.

5 Look at the circle below.

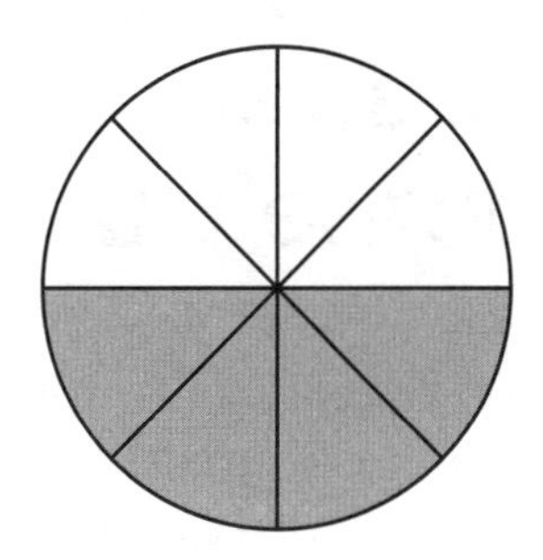

A What fraction of the circle is shaded?

Answer: ___________

B Write an equivalent fraction in fourths.

Answer: ___________

6 Andy ate $\frac{1}{2}$ of a sandwich, Philip ate $\frac{1}{4}$ of a sandwich, and Miguel ate $\frac{1}{3}$ of a sandwich.

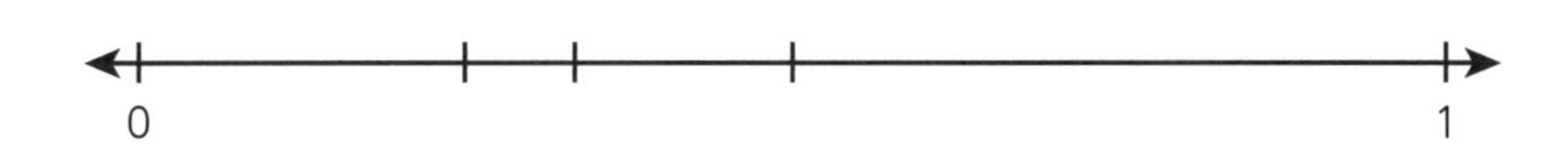

A Write $\frac{1}{2}$, $\frac{1}{4}$, and $\frac{1}{3}$ under the correct marks on the number line above.

B Who ate the ***smallest*** fraction of sandwich, Andy, Philip, or Miguel?

Answer: ______________________

C Explain how you know your answer is correct.

____

____

____

How to Answer Constructed Response Questions

Many test items are multiple-choice items. Usually, a multiple-choice question offers four answer choices to pick from, and you must select the best one. Constructed response items are different. They are questions that you must answer in your own words, in writing. Constructed response items test more than just math content skills. These items tell if you can **represent** mathematical ideas and understand how they **connect.** They show if you can **reason** why something works or is true. They allow you to **communicate** what you know. And they let you demonstrate your **problem-solving** skills.

Constructed response items may be short or long. Sometimes a question asks for a **short response,** which will have two parts. Usually the first part asks you to solve a problem and show your work. It could be computing some numbers, working out an equation, or drawing a diagram. In the second part you may have to identify the correct answer and perhaps explain why the answer is correct or how you found it.

Other constructed response items call for an **extended response.** These problems are often like the short response items, but they have more steps or are more difficult. Many times the question starts with one problem. When you have solved that part, more information is added. You use the new information to solve a second part. Just as with short response items, you need to explain how you found your solution. These questions focus on problem solving.

To do a good job answering constructed response questions, follow these tips:

- Read the problem carefully to be sure you understand what it is asking. Follow the directions exactly.
- Remember the four steps for solving problems: read, plan, solve, and check.
- If you are asked to show your work, show every step neatly and label the answer.
- Think about what you want to say *before* you write an explanation. Organize your thoughts. Then write clearly so anyone can understand what you have to say.